Books by Dabney Stuart

The Diving Bell
1966

A Particular Place
1969

These are Borzoi Books,
published in New York by
Alfred A. Knopf

A Particular Place

A Particular Place

Poems by Dabney Stuart

Alfred A. Knopf   New York   1969

7/1970
Eng.

This is a Borzoi Book
published by Alfred A. Knopf, Inc.

Some of the poems in this collection
first appeared in The Kenyon Review, Jeopardy, The Southern Review,
Poetry, The Denver Quarterly, Poetry Northwest, Lillabulero, Panache,
Shenandoah, The New Orleans Review, *and* The Malahat Review.
"The Drowning" first appeared in The New Yorker.

For Martha, my wife

Contents

I Sources

"*We have been privileged to look for nothing,*

   And it is right that we return
   To exit where we entered, nothing in our hands."
                —HOWARD NEMEROV

His Third Decade

1

Ends in a house
Collapsing into itself

Whatever direction the wind takes
There is a wall to receive it

Caught inside
At the last moment

The moment where four winds meet
And the walls give in
To what is beyond them

He finds himself
Unsafe anywhere
But tries the basement stairs, going
Down.

2

Ends on another flight
Beginning in wreckage

Going down from the moment
Where four winds met
No more than another frame
House already drawing in
Toward the one small life

His life

Which had never been
More than one place at a time.

3

Ends at the one small place
He had from the beginning

The winds' focus
To which the walls had fallen

Himself

Descending now beneath the foundation
He finds room enough

Meets all his fathers
In the taproot of an oak

Moves upward again through them
Into the winds   his brothers

Remembering it

As the bole expands
He counts the rings of his self
Collects the years, like bark

Lives here, lives
Here, giving this wood his name

Calling it home.

Love Song

When I was dying
I held the lamp as high as my feet

Looking down out of the darkness
I saw where I could walk

Saw for the first time
How the path made its own way

If I had waited a hundred times
Or until my feet froze to the light

I would have covered the same ground
Met myself at the same edges

Offered my friends the same scraps
Of a dream they could not assemble

I ask you friends
Do you hear the sound of our feet

Shuffling this puzzle
And the sound of someone scraping

As though digging a well
Burying a bone

Planting a seed
In this troubled radiance?

Hunter, Prey

Downwind, he caught the scent
Coming from where he had been

Turning
He waited for it to approach him

It covered his tracks
Bearing his prime intent
Until it stood where he stood

He recognized the place

The wind lifted to a great height
Trembling the roots of an aspen

And the sun focused through him
As through a lens

A stone burned with the light

The Drowning

I thought it was late
So I took the shadows two at a time.
I made it to the edge of the last one
When the conductor yelled *All overboard*.

It was deep enough.

On the way down
I passed two hands holding each other
The inside of a leaf
My own face reflected on a stone.

I carried it with me.

Everyone said it was a perfect likeness
But when I kissed it
It tasted of salt.
This isn't anyone I know I kept saying
Until I understood the back of its eyes
And knew it was weeping.

I thought that was the bottom

But found myself
Climbing over the far edge of the shadow
Clutching a blank stone
Holding my breath in a new country.

The Well

I noticed first the moss covering the anchor
Then the way it filled the gaps between the stones
Like mortar.
Around the clearing the foliage was dense as a wall
I could smell mint and hear streams in the distance
Carrying on.
A piece of sky hung above me, like a wafer.

No one came except Bones, the janitor,
And he came every day regular as the tide.
He hadn't changed.
His good eye was deep enough to drop a bucket into
And his glass one gave back everything.

I could see I was still there.

He dropped the anchor all the way
Until he couldn't hear anything.
More rope he said
And loped off through the fern
Climbed the trees top to top like stone stairs
And disappeared with both eyes over the edge.

I hauled up the anchor
Feeling its weight in my bones
It rang against the sides like a muffled clapper
My eyes crossed with the strain
I almost fell in getting the thing over the rim.

Bones hasn't come back yet
And my eyes are still crossed
But I swear
There's a drop of water
On one tip of the anchor.

Forget the rope, Bones,
We made it.
Get me that wafer.

Bridge

He held one suit; it was black.
To himself he called it what it was.
All its edges were sharp
Even at arm's length.
It repeated itself one end to the other.

He remembered the groundbreaking
The hole deepening
The arc of clods
The mound rising
The chink chink of the metal's bidding.

Come on he heard across the board
Open.

He felt his lie pulse in his fingers
Spanning the deadpan backs of the cards.

One heart he said
One heart

Quarry

Her breath sounded like dogs whining
Far off.

       She welcomed me.

I came through the parted curtain
And removed her trophies.

The bare walls seemed to sing
Suddenly there were windows
The wind turned

We cast the only shadows

One shadow
Bidding the hunter farewell
From the lighted sill.

Love Letter

He found
A single feather in the sprung trap

He took it home
And with it
Wrote to his wife

I make this with part of what escaped
You know the style

I have always imagined
A calendar retrieving its pages

A stone house with a spring
A rune scratched on a wall in its cellar
A hearth

The light here quivers
As if the wind were in it

I make this with part of what is free

When he gave it to her
She said, without reading it

I have something to show you

Come to the window

High Wire

All the way he heard someone breathing

It seemed he walked that breathing
As toward the source of a wind
Or a far voice echoing

He looked back once
The place where he began followed him

I'm not getting anywhere he said
And saw he was closer

He was the focus of distances
He stood still and heard the same space
Balancing

When I come to the end he thought
I will turn around and say   Here

Take my hand

The Cage

He didn't notice it when he moved
Because it moved with him

But it portioned his stillness

Always the light
Seemed broken

When he spoke
The echoes were partial

Whichever way he looked
People disappeared
As though into their names

He reached out
And was burned

Drank the water from his blisters

When he saw his own face in his scars
He knew
That the strings which enclosed him
Kept the song he had forgotten

Asked him only that he give them his fingers
And come in

Power Failure

for Dan Hoffman

Somewhere the lines were down
He imagined the current expiring
Into the loose wind
Thrilling the darkness

His legs carried him to a candle
Its light moved
Breathing the dry air

I'll check the fuses he said
To be sure   ·
And descended the long flight
Into stone

Beneath seasons
He found it cold
Did not remember the moisture
Nor the brute drawings
Flickering on the walls

When his fingers responded
He dropped the candle

Went by touch

His fingers fitting their prints

He was without direction
Following a vein in the rock
Did not know
When he passed through the crevice
Too small for his breath

And discovered himself
Kissing his wrists in a morning
Stunned by his bones' brightness.

The Return

He'd had enough
Of the patterns of heroes
—The epic river
The descent into voices
The crisp symbol cast on a new shore—

Was done with disguises

Came home like any man
Stripped of his gifts
Derelict

And found the same door
He had always been entering

The same dead in the keyhole
The same shadows shaping the light
The same leak in the mirror

My people he said
And they said *My people*

The words danced on the threshold
Like grain in the wind
And when they bowed
He bowed.

Story

I walk through impossible rooms

Where my sister asks
If she must go carefully on the mountains
When it is time

Where my brother begins
Hearing the wind
Trouble the far side of the aspen

Where my wives keep house among stones
Listening for their children

Where my mother does not take sides
Preferring to wear her pain like flesh
Her bones find their burden every morning

Where my father turns toward a light
Focusing
As if to a diamond

Where the shape of a beast
Surprises my groping
In every darkness I choose

Sequel
Somewhere beyond each hide
He hears that which moves
In him and out of him,
Singing,
Ascending.

II   Notes

*"[I] find that all things stedfastnes doe hate
And changed be . . .*

I Love You

It's hard to say that to you,
To anybody,
But I do.

Often I have sprawled under the table
Ordering messages among the crumbs
And been satisfied
While you, and you, and anybody
Laughed as you latched a door
Behind you in the distance.
Sometimes I have had
A whole house to myself. In those cities
No ceilings were too high
No risk too clean, no work
Too difficult. Then I could say
Anything, and did. Doors kept
Locking and unlocking to the echoes
I hardly heard, blessing
My ears and hallways, each fresh sound
Hanging around its mute catastrophe.
It was as if the mail would never come,
I'd never have to watch a telegram
Grate under the door
Reminding me of secrets and sealed things,
Who owned this house
And who was here, and wasn't.

When I began
To go outdoors again I tried on stars
In lieu of you-know-what. I was
No slim effete, knew right away
Just how that getup fit. Old baggy pants.
So where was I to go? Back to my crumbs,
The trite hosannas on my bathroom walls,
The private kitchen of my peas and cues?
I did, and what a hash I'd made

Of that. So *To the roof* I cried
Like Caesar, mad for war, and hoped for birds
Like Francis, strictly. I had the crust.

On top at last, I looked both up and down,
The world, or something similar, to execute.
The clouds shaped up. I was Polonius:
Oh very like. A whale, leviathan,
Cast off from sea to sea.
                                    I'm sick of this
I thought. *I've been around.* And two things
Happened.
This bird, or very like a bird, hooked
Talons to my hands. I grounded him,
Hung on. And in the park
I bought balloons, hung on to them.

You find me like this, minion, an octopus
Hanging on, up to no good, needing
You. Don't cut the strings. I swear
There's weight enough for two. Please help
Me navigate this foolish ground.

Worldly Goods

I kiss you: like this.
If I say your lips are petals
I mean only that I kiss a flower:
Like this
Crocus
Which blooms so close to the ground
I have to lie full length on the ground
To kiss it:
Like this.

If, kissing you, I say
Your lips are soft as breezes
I mean only that I kiss the air:
Like this
Air
We breathe into each other's mouths, this
Air that God knows
What other mouths have breathed
And flowers kissed
And mouths flowered:
Like this.

When I kiss you like
This flower breathes
My body full length on the earth
Whose blooming mouths
Kiss the air we breathe
If I say I kiss you, I mean:
Like this.

Anniversary

Our first year turns. Were this another age
I'd have figures ready-made
And wouldn't have to think up how to say
The sun could warm the world by circling us,
The bands upon our fingers tune the spheres,
Two Adams treat us with a single tree
Whose apple falls through darkness into light.

But it's been done. Since then the years
Have turned more than two hundred times
Shucking the terms that served more faithful men
Than I was, before I married you. You bring
A warmth and music
Those fond conceits don't suit, and yet
I would have you know,
Lady,
Wife of my turning years,
There's never a heathen lout in Christendom
Would not be saved by that fidelity
I bear you pared and glistening, like a fruit.

Commonplace

Seeing you seated across this room,
The firelight troubled
On the porcelain vase beside you
As foliage moves under a light breeze
Evenings, I wonder at space

Not that distance where
Gasses toss off their simple blooms
Into thin air,
Where the unmeasured stones
Fade from themselves, or burst, and disappear

But here, between you
And me where the pressure is
Greater, where the force
Which holds us to our local sphere
Accommodates a vase of roses
A hearth, a chair,
Keeps the pieces of what we break
Within reach, in our own atmosphere.

Five Women Seen as Figures in a Tapestry

1

She has been looking at something
Either in the past or beyond the border
For her eyes—the blue threads
Are slightly frayed—seem to have settled
Only at this moment
On the objects in the grass before her:
A child's fiddle, three pins
Fallen from her hair, and a gold coin
In which she sees her face.

2

She is the only one standing,
And seems composed
Of three directions: the line,
Taut as a bowstring, from her heels
To her neck, the tense curve
Of her arms reaching toward a blank place
In the cloth, and the tilt of her head
Downward toward her elbows.
Balanced in the crotch of a bare tree behind her
Is a small blue egg.

3

She kneels, washing her hair
In a pool of the same color.
There is no reflection, and above her
A butterfly seems to disappear.

4

She seems to be reading.
The perspective is odd
For the book is as large as she is
And on the page which she is turning
She appears turning the page
Of an outsize book she seems to be
Reading. She is the only nude
And her skin, as far as the threads
Allow it, has the smoothness of snow.

5

She is older than the others
And is shown petting
An indistinguishable object
—An animal, the china cast
Of an animal—in her lap.
She seems to be waiting
For the coming of an expected season.

6

They are arranged in a circle
Whose center is a rib
Bearing the signature of the weaver.

Lines

You sing in my lap
In your daylight sleep,
One finger jogging the tune
In the air while the train
Wheels hum and clack
To their beaten track.

When I was your singing age
A fireman earned his wage
Keeping the pressure up.
We're diesel and wider gauge
Now, for our yearly trip.
We move from stage to stage.

I saw you every day
Once, before you and your mother
Went your own way.
Though your other
Weaning was slower, you left the breast
And eat in the diner now, my guest.

By night you've sung
Yourself awake.
You remind me of the trout
I caught which began our week,
And say it's wrong
To use live bait.

The lights by the rails slow down
As your mother waves
Us in. Through the train
Window I promise to save
You a week the next July.
You wave goodbye.

Goodbye; now I'll go back
To the end of the line
Where I live, and learn
To tie
An artificial fly
Which hides the hook.

Confirmation

for my daughter, as the mysteries increase

1 The World

First of all, it's out there
As the name *star* or *daughter* or *eye* is out there
When you hear it spoken
Or see it printed
Or think it.

Then, there are edges.
It's a long way from your eye to a star
From father to daughter
But everything touches.
That is why space.
That is why God drinks from a glass.
That is why the name for what you grow in
Is *time.*
That is why you can't tell
Where darkness ends and light begins
Or the other way round.
That is *why,*
Edges.

Something else is where we go
When we forget.
It is a short distance
Like the distance between your thumb and your thumbnail
Or between your eye and a star.
If you look at your thumb
Through the wrong end of a telescope
You will begin to see.
You have to forget to begin to see.
Then you remember.

Remembering and forgetting get to be the same place.

There isn't much to be said for winning.
You just stand there holding your prizes.
I knew a man who never forgot
Because he won so many prizes.

One more thing:
I said the world's out there
But I should have said you carry it inside you, too.
Remember the edges
And the way you can't tell
When winter ends and winter begins
Or how close a star is
Or how far it is to yourself
Or how much you discover when you lose,
Like Columbus.

What you have to do is be ready
To touch everything
Inside out.

2   The Flesh

You can touch with this
If you remember
It's not the only thing.

3   The Devil

He is another language, like God.
What he means gets lost in translation.

Some say he has horns
But a cornucopia is a horn
And other horns make music.

Maybe when people say he has horns
They mean he is *too much*
Or that he dances to a tune
Only the sharpest ears know
As a dog hears a whistle
Beyond us.

Then *The devil has horns* is a translation of
He is the edge we are afraid of.

If you go back far enough
You'll learn *horn* and *head*
Grew from the same root,
And *we* have heads.
So *The devil has horns* may be an address.

Others say he has cloven hooves.
Remember that when you kick up your heels.

And when the traces go over
With a clatter and you bound
As free as the Equator
Across the field through the Paradise trees
If you meet something that crosses you
—Maybe a high stile
Or a bed of thistles
Or a deep creek
Where you see your reflection—
Then you will know what *devil* means
In your own language.

Since you can't tell a soul
The only thing to do then
Is what you do for the world and your flesh:
Love him to death.

Sunburst

A friend writes
How's the prince?
I bet he's a pisser.

He is.
Anywhere:
In his bath
Naked under the sun
Getting his pants changed
The sudden burst
The rise
The high peak
And the fall.

Not a word
But this bow
Warm as spring rain
Rainbow
Pot of gold
Dazzling
Curve of the world.

When he grows up
May he find
Such light
Such shape
Such perfect levity
For what he can't use.

The Student

Under the rusting elms his separate path
Crossing and recrossing the separate paths
Of others like himself, whose aimless feet
Weave some invisible pattern on the grass,
Takes him to his classroom, to his seat,
Where he walks on words toward a drowning man
He dimly imagines, or pictures in vague dreams,
A shifty man whose face he thinks familiar
As his own, yet cannot fix exactly,
Who calls to him when he walks out again
Onto the solid earth to thread his way
Under the rusting elm leaves, which float down
Like nets through water seeking the vagrant school.

The Leaf-Eater

The wind-sacked beast
Chugs and whines across the campus lawn
Sucking up the leaves in ordered rows
Before the first freeze and the winter snows.
A man says to himself, stifling a yawn,
They seem to have fallen for this raucous feast.

He watches from his office. Since quitting-time
Last night dogwood and elm did as they always do,
Dropping what was lifeless, coming clean,
While that machine
Cooled off in the shed, deflated and askew,
Hungover from its swinish pantomime.

But, again this morning, swollen like a sow,
It gorges on dead leaves, and its own noise,
So loud his thoughts go haywire. The childish
Fantasies he had cast off as trash
Heap up, tempting his windy hunger. A voice
Says *Eat,* and he fills the vacuum made by his old vow

To think austerely, dropping his green schemes.
Though dry at first, this fare
Suddenly turns sumptuous as spring
Beneath whose trees, ardent and flourishing,
The ghost of a boy turns cartwheels, unaware
He lives beyond the seasons of his dreams.

The Cooks

Jerry: Salads

Late at night, when you got back to your one-room
Cabin in the woods, you never turned on the light
But felt your way to your bed by the nude-postered walls.
I used to sneak in there in the daytime, and don't remember
Seeing a grain of wood, except when I looked at my feet.
Imagining your bedtime trip, I wondered if the walls
Held you up, or you the walls.
Then I would sit on the bed in your little everywhere
And mess up my sleep that night, while you mixed salads
In the mess hall for my supper—cucumbers, radishes, lettuce,
Head and heart.
                    Back in my cabin after taps, the walls
All wood but my mind a film of breasts and thighs and asses,
I'd toss awake, mixed up almost to dawn,
And as I moved into a dream of sleep, or sleep,
I'd hear you rise from your bed, throw on a towel
And walk through the forty-degree morning down to the river,
Hear you throw cold water across your back
And laugh like hell until the river sang on its stones
And the mountains leapt like fish through the mist
And the sun swelled like a teat in your hand.

Jack: Meats

Your bloodshot eyes at five
In the morning were maps
Of a cracked continent,
Highways of lust and jive

You'd driven to the laps
Of more women than God sent
Solomon. But you survived
Those nightly trips

By craft or accident
And were back at your stove
Cleaning the grease traps
Early, following each carouse

By roasting meat
All day for two hundred boys
Until, cook's choice,
It was bloodless from the heat.

A Gesture

for C. H. S. (1879–1953)

I remember you bowed,
Grandmother: over the stove
Tending the dough you leavened
Into bread; over the bed you made
Tucking the cornered sheets
Precisely under the mattress
You died on; over your husband
Kissing goodnight those lips
Which muttered the market page
Reports as you left the room;
And at grace before meals
The words so much your own
They spoke themselves,
Blessing you.

As though life itself were a feast
You were obedient to
You bowed to it each time you moved,
Leavening us, giving rise
To a silent order we could dream
In the beds we made.
And here, tonight, cornered by distances
Husbands and wives expand
As they reach over,
I ask that you take my bow
Not to a name, but to your human grace.

The Fisherman

*Alcemon, a pupil of Pythagoras, thought
that men die because they cannot join their
beginning and their end.*

—W. B. YEATS

Thick water laps
The seawall's edge as the tide ebbs,
Leaving its stain
On the shelved, gray stone.
Out past the shallows where crabs
Eke trails nobody maps

My sinker nudges the ooze.
Above it two barbed hooks
Wave in the current like weeds.
On this end of the line I practice tricks
To convince some sucker fish he needs
To play this game of what we've got to lose.

All day on the stone wall
And nothing's worked. The same cheap shrimp
I started with slog beyond the shoals,
Going nowhere. Long past cramps
Numb to my nape, in the ebbing light
I'm caught. How does a hooked man fight?

The thick dark flows around me half asleep:
Sparrows peck dung in a green street.
Gulls, hung above a liner's stern like kites,
Scrounge garbage. Vultures, who know their rights,
Pluck out a dead man's eyes. A winding sheet
Unrolls a sailor's body, lets it drop.

I wake. Though bottom-blind, afraid
These waters might yield
A catch so rich and strange that I could wield
It no better than my dreams, I wait
For whatever spawn or breed
Will take my bait.

Spring Song

This month swelltoads begin to run,
Not as shad run, bearing their spawn
Lightly, smoothly, nor as the bluefish slides
Dreamlike through his own
Dream, but as a stone in mud
Moves, or does not move, as the drift decides.

This month—this April—some toad begins again
His awkward run over the stones and mud
He looks like, taking in
Through a mouth whose solid bone
Seems made to break stone
Whatever keeps him going. Though the hook
That takes a shad lightly, smoothly, cannot crack
That mouth, he will be caught, will swell
On land into a perfect ball,
Will ride in his death the press
Of his belly as white
As a virgin's breast,
And the fisherman will find
The meat inside as white
As milk, as sweet
To his mouth as to a mind
That has fed on mud and stones
A song can be, sung in the bones.

Right of Way

to Randall Jarrell

*Poetry, art—these too are occupations of a sort; and
I do not recommend them to you any more than I recommend to you that, tonight, you go home to bed, and
go to sleep, and dream.*

—R. J.

The day I heard about your suicide
I went numb as a bird's bill,
And saw your singing
Splattered on the highway
And the dumb grill of the car
You stepped in front of.
                    I cried.
I taught a class. I wrote your name
On the blackboard. I went for a drive
Right down the center line, watching for
Pedestrians. A cardinal
On the shoulder flew into my wheel
For his own reasons. I saw him twitch
In the rear view mirror. By the time
I stopped and went back, he'd died.

Now at night a dream I can't scare off
Bears down on me:
A red bird sits on some groundless ground nowhere
Preening, singing soundlessly into his wing,
Impossibly proud, so self-contained
His color alone drives me broad awake.

Exchange

It's always there, like the drone
I hear when I pick up the telephone,
Steady, uninsistent, satisfied
With never having made a vow or lied
Or done anything, in fact, but been
Around, ubiquitous, yet mine.
The wish to die, I mean.

It's always there, like the drone
I hear when the voice at the other end
Hangs up, having said it all
For once. As long as I hang on no other call
Can break through to me, standing alone.
I have to dial to hide that constant tone.
The fear of death, I mean.

Fit

I saw your arm rise
Like a cobra from the basket
Of your body, writhe
To its own music,
Your fingers hooking like fangs,
Your head jolting against the back
Of your seat, your eyes hung on something
You didn't see
Behind you, over your shoulder.
I saw your long arm gnarl,
Your fingers stricken limbs
Of a lightning tree.

Flutist and snake, fire and bole,
Your strange arm danced
On its wordless poison
Like a signal, while you gargled
Your tongue and watched
Whatever it was over your shoulder.

After the rescue squad
Wheeled you away, the show
Went on and I saw
On stage a hundred girls swaying
And whirling, their fragile arms
Flung upward and upward
Into the fabulous lights,
Their charming heads
Wordlessly turning and turning,
The ancient music
Playing and playing, on and on and on.

Cat Eyes: A Geometry Problem

You look through me when you look at me,
As if you see something behind my head
I never see—when I look in the mirror
To catch whatever's back there that catches your eye,
My head gets in the way—

You look into yourself when you look at me—
When I try to follow your gaze that way,
Drawing close to your eyes,
I find my own reflection;

The focus of longing inside you
Diverges a long distance
Until it moves through your eyes
And draws together again
Into the focus of sadness before you;

Sometimes when I look at you
I remember driving a long way once, at night,
Wanting to get home,
When a stray cat appeared from nowhere, and froze
Before me, blinded in the focus of my lights:

When I stopped and walked back
I found it quivering two distances together in its eyes
Until there was only the one still, lightless place.

III Rockbridge Poems

"*I am certain that a man should find his Holy Land where he first crept upon the floor, and that familiar woods and rivers should fade into symbol with so gradual a change that he may never discover, no, not even in ecstasy itself, that he is beyond space.*"

—W. B. YEATS

Middle-Atlantic States

On the coast of Maryland, a landing place
    —Say at Willows, Plum Point,
    Dares—the promises of saint
And settler keep themselves. Week after week
Late August and September, croppers, for a price,
Harvest the weed that shores the Chesapeake.

In mind of another coast, some port of call
    —Say Accra, Dakar,
    Sassandra—your tired, your poor
Eke out their shadows from the going rate.
Mise en scene: a summer house, a sail,
A scepter, the shape of dreams, a cigarette.

In western Virginia, wind-scraped, mountainous
    —Say at Wintergreen, Crows,
    Goshen—nothing much grows.
The houses lived in year-round stand
    Where they were raised,
    Reeving these untenanted lands.

Highways

Three of them split the Valley now: Parkway,
Eleven, Interstate. The high-speed card
The driver buys, after his exit, shows
Lilac, dogwood, rhododendron, bay.

Each mile he's placed exactly. Verdant signs
Omit those towns, fabled, beyond his grade,
Beyond the margin of his chartered lanes:
Mt. Olive, Palos, Singers Glen, Parnassus.
North-south, south-north, he takes his means and ends.

Either way, he's driven by the number;
Blue shield, white shield, windshield, the way it goes.
The blind map in his glove-compartment reads
Allegheny, Blue Ridge, Shenandoah.

The Maury River

The Commodore's charts did not include
   This narrow, inland whim—
The river where his name is moored.
   Beside its autumn scum

A boy and a girl play catch, the ball
   Black in the twilit air
Marking a passage with each rise and fall.
   The river, rising higher

At April thaw, will flood this shore
   Warm for that distant swell
Where Maury patterned a career
   Shadowed by his sail.

The nameless pair whose local games
   Find out a darker strand
Feel playing on their sun-tanned limbs
   A wind from Port Etienne.

Rockbridge Baths

On the highway through the town
The speed limit has been
Raised to 45

Forty-five years ago sons and daughters
Whose lives were a vacation, who didn't dream
Their fathers' dreams, came to this dream
This rockbound fountain of startling waters.

Part of the old road
Has gone to seed,
A weedy drive

They drove here, by motorcar or carriage
Parking in fields, following stony paths
Barefoot from the hotel, walking to the baths
Keeping their balance on the swinging bridge.

These days most of the men
Commute to Staunton, Lexington,
Making ends
Meet, staying alive

The springs are still alive.
They have been channeled to the Maury
Or run off underground, as if to say
What has been forgotten will be served.

Jump Mountain

Natives here have seen
Curious fishermen,
Hip-deep in the stream
At its base, look
From their empty creels
Up that slow incline
And miss their strikes,
Or hunters, sighting that peak
As they raise the blued steel
To the spraying coveys, stand
Still as does, and lose their game.

There is nothing up there to explain
This, nothing but stone
And the sharp drop
To stone on the other side
Which an Indian prince and his bride
Made their marriage bed,
Nothing to stop
Civilized sport, to keep
The barbed hook from the bass
Or lead from the quail.

At the edge of Goshen Pass,
In Rockbridge Baths, the trail
Begins—an easy climb
Past maple, pine and elm,
Past blueberry and scrub oak
Whose twisted maze rattlesnakes
Solve with the ease of dreams,
Taking their prey—an easy climb
To nothing but stone
And a sharp drop
To stone: a notion, a name.

Birds at Timber Ridge

The farmer has said their names
To himself, standing alone
In the half-plowed furrow they cross
Above him, cross and recross
Leaving no trace, the air
Closing behind them where they were.

He has said their names
Stopping, easing the strain
On his dried-up traces, his shoe
Touching a turned-up stone,
Still in the line of stones
Behind him, where he has been.

And their names
Have crossed his dreams
Stood still in his half-plowed head
Lodged there, like stones:
Waxwing, quail, mockingbird,
Killdeer, mourning-dove, crow.

Goshen Pass: Winter

for Henry Sloss

Seen through the windshield of a car
Winding from one end of this pass to the other
The mountains seem to move, as a half-open door
Moves when you move, revealing more, or less,
Of the room beyond it. Yet the man who starts in this pass
Walking
Finds his hike entirely mountainous
Finds nothing he did not see from his car,
Though he may learn that if the mountains move
He does not move them.
      Seen through the windshield of a car
Parked anywhere in this pass
Sheer rhododendron, bare oak
And dogwood, the monotonous evergreens
Cedar and fir, all seem rooted in stone
Shelf after shelf. Gross limpet shells
Of ice suck the receding ledges
Where fold and scarp poise upward on themselves
To the high ridges. Yet the man who sits in this pass
Staring, is blind
To this, the face of it

The way the mountains move

And in a time that is beyond his means
They will have outstripped his climbing, moved to a height
Visible only from the single island
Poised in the river moving over its stones
—the stones of the mountains—its singing caught
By the walls of its passage, increased,
As though it were tuned to their motion
As well as its own.
     And spring,
That dubious season, has nothing to do with this motion,
Will not in his time bring
Either delicate feet to these raw terraces

Subduing them, or those others rehearsing their ring
Who come to bless stone, and whom stone blesses.

For now, this is his pass
And he has come to it with his boots on
Faithful to his season, a driving age
Whose ghosts will not be seen dancing beneath that tree
Stone-rooted on the solitary island, willing a heritage
Of celebration and austerity.
Whatever he sees now he sees for the same reason
That the clearest pane of glass
May show him
Not the aspect of a particular place
But only, reflected, his own face.

IV   Patterns

> . . . *yet being rightly wayd*
> *They are not changed from their first estate;*
> *But by their change their being doe dilate:*
> *And turning to themselves at length againe,*
> *Doe worke their owne perfection so by fate.* ''
> —EDMUND SPENSER

Buildings

for Dale Richardson

I have come home again.
Or—how would you put it?—
Back to the house I live in five days a week.
Frame, marking a hillside six miles from town.
I have heard it said
A house, rightly inhabited, becomes one's signature.
I wish the corners of my name
Bore the midnight's cutting winds as well as this house.
Then I would move it to the top of a mountain
Stone by stone.
         Another legend
Tells of a house whose stones numbered its age.
Each year it stood
Its foundation increased by one stone at the bottom.
A man could spend his life
Digging for the last of those stones,
A kind of homecoming.

         But I am here.
The shovel rusts among cobwebs in the shed
And the floors creak when the furnace goes on.
It is the sort of night one goes down to the lake
And skips gravel on the moonlit water
Imagining the pebbles sinking
Slowly,
One
By
One
Into the darkness
Until, with luck or a fly fisherman's skill,
One knows he has made them settle
Into the walls of a house.

         But I stay here
Having already come home once tonight,
Thinking of a poem of careful numbers—five
Days, six

Miles, seventeen
Years of locusts—
Which add up to my age,
A poem which ends with my name,
A house on a hill.

Turning the furnace down, I go to bed.
Like stones into water
All my years
Settle slowly into a dream.

The Charles River

Cambridge: from the Cowley Fathers' Monastery

1

On Memorial Drive, outside the cloister wall,
The sycamores peel: there a layer
Beneath a layer beneath
A layer of bark,
Hinting a way inside.

I was told there are people inside
The cloister. I
Never saw a soul, and I
Used to walk often under those sycamores
Beside the river. The shadows
Cast by their limbs at night
Were the same as the shadows their limbs cast
By day: there a shadow
Beneath a shadow, shadowed.

2

Their faces would come toward me
Day and night: the mother
From the park, a student
Under the influence of Thoreau,
A clerk from the Coop, off-duty,
The full professor whose eyes
Lay open like a book face down on a table.

If I were to dream one face
Approaching me under the sycamores
Beside the river, it would be
Her face beneath his face beneath
Her face. It would be

A manner of seeing
As a dream is, as a poem is
A manner of speaking,
A shadow, a way inside.

3

We walk there, I
And the faces which come toward me,
Beside the river beneath the sycamores
Where others sit on their books
Reading the water the way a child
Watches its grandmother crochet a shawl.

Perhaps those people inside the cloister
Hear rumors of all this, perhaps
They watch from their casements
The water through the sycamores.
Perhaps all of us together
Have looked once on the river
Beneath the shadows of those trees
Where all is dark, and seen
It take us in.

Boston: from the Embankment

1

On summer evenings here
Lovers may kiss to Stravinsky:
Le sacre du printemps.
If they lie close enough
To the bank, the music and the river
Lapping the stones
Become one sound, one
Sound also with the beat
Of the ducks' wings flying

Above the lovers, the ducks' wings folding
As they settle on the lagoon,
Heart of the city.

2

There is an instant, a point of turning
When a duck seems poised
On the tip of one wing, a point of
Turning before the settling in.
He seems to sail then,
His wing taking the air
As those white sails take it
Into themselves, filling,
Moving the shells over the water
With the swiftness of birds.

With the swiftness of fish
The shell moves under the water
The fin of its sail filled,
Taut, still, yet moving, pointed down,
Its tip a point of turning.
The sail over the river, the sail
Beneath it, the wing of the duck's poise
Above it move the world
Moves on the point of its turning.

3

I have known it
Become a matter of names:
Brimmer, the filled glass—
The singing blossom, Chestnut and Spruce and Lime—
An old warning, Revere,
And two chimes ringing—

The Union Boat Club,
Hatch Memorial Shell:
Matter and names, yolk and white
In the one shell, hatching

A manner of speaking
As a poem is, as a dream is
A manner of seeing

As the dream of a poem
Hears the one sound
The rites of spring beating their wings
Above the lovers, the music
Lapping the stones, the river
Kissing the down
Down of the ducks, coming in

Or as the poem of a dream
Imagines a wing
A white sail
A fin
And cannot tell
Whether the river reflects
The white wing beating,
The sail rippling, or the air
Reflects the white sail rippling,
The deep fin beating,
And cannot tell
Which part of the one world
Watches itself, as Narcissus watched
Himself from the depth of his longing
And his loveliness until it took him in.

Sticks and Stones

This pencil moves on the page
White as a swan's quill,
Making its music,
Playing its tunes
With no more noise than a swan
Makes moving
Over the rippling lake.

Three hundred years ago
Men wrote
With the feathers of birds
And courtly fingers
Picked Morley's airs
From the lute with plectra
Made from the feathers of birds.

This pencil, Venus 2,
This unwieldy timber
You can start a fire with,
This shaving
That writes *tree,*
This small stick
That bears the name of a goddess
And can write *love*
As cleanly as a knife
Cuts the names of lovers
Into the bark of trees,
This light toy
That can form a word
Heavy as *stone,*
Leaves its marks on this white paper

With no more noise
Than a pebble
Thrown by two lovers
In late afternoon
Makes, sinking
Through the water
Of a lake, played on
By the shadows of trees.

3

The river in its narrows
Moves on over the stones,
Riffles, moves on over
The stones, reflects the sun,
Moves on, covering the stones
Played on by the shadows of trees.

A fisherman's rod
Moves through its arc, the fly
Settles on the water,
Drifts through the sun,
Plays in the shadows of trees,
Moves on over the stones
To the end of the line, jerks,
Drifts, jerks.

The fisherman's blood
Hums in its veins,
Moves on over his bones.

4

The small-mouth bass
Hovers over the pebbles
In the moving water,
Watching the fly jerk,

Drift, jerk.
Dappled, motionless
As a stone, he waits
On his hunger, and will rise
For the fly in one
Invisible swiftness,
As the fisherman's need
Rises silently to words
Through the depths of his dreams.

5

Scattered along the shore
Among the stones
Untouched by the water
The bones of birds
Lie, bleached whiter
Than this page, played on
By the shadows of trees.

6

Above the still lake water
And the moving stream,
Above their beds of stones,
The wings of birds
Make no more noise
Than this pencil moving
Across this page, leaving
Its weight of words,
Make no more noise
Than the bass striking
The fly, no more
Than the fly drifting,
Jerking, drifting, no
More than the fisherman's need

Rising through his sleep
Leaving his dreams
Through words that seem
In their silence
To fly under the sun
Nest in the shadows of trees.

To His Father, Dying

Whether under bright sun or in darkness
It is not necessary to remember
Nor is it necessary to recall the shadows
Or account for them if they were there
For it is all the same
In this phase of the dream

Whether it was a descent or an ascent
It is not fruitful to ask
Whether the stone slope led down to the river
Or by the chance of another measure
Led upward to it
In this phase of the dream
Is all the same

See, they depart, and we go with them.

I want to say it was timeless
But it was not
Because there was motion

I want to say it was spaceless
But it was not
Because there was motion

We moved towards
As if there were something we were leaving
We moved from
As if there were a destination

I would say
Time and space
We never understood

Had become the sources
Of their own dissolution

The place to which we moved
—The river, the shore of the river—
Was where we had started

The place we had left was before us

See, they depart, and we go with them.

Two forms
Waited at the edge of the river

We sat into them

I was awake to our danger

Flung my arm across my face
Turned aside from the breaker

Reached but did not reach
To protect you sitting beside me

Beyond my reach

And the moment the breaker
Submerged us

I saw your arms folded on your chest
Your face raised

Smiling

See, they depart, and we go with them.

We breed and conclude
In the marriage bed
Leave and enter
At the same center

Before and after

Dread and need
Nourish the seed

Blossom and stem
Share one name

Now and then

Who can own
His flesh and bone

Lose his ghost
Bury his dust

Here and there

See, they depart, and we go with them.

Is it that I want
What you want
Because I cannot replace you

Has my son
Made me your son,
The fruit remembering only
Its own season?

Is it that what you want
Is what I have wanted for you
Before this, before I had seen you oppose it

Are the opposition and the defeat
One,
The blood in the vein
Inscribing the stone?

Is it that I know
What you have known
And forgotten

Do not need to know anymore
Because I know it,
The mourner mourning himself
At his father's stone?

Is it that I do not know
What you know,
Your stone echoing my name
Your blood dreaming my dream?

If there is an answer

See, they depart, and we go with them.

A Note About the Author

DABNEY STUART was born in Richmond, Virginia, in 1937, and grew up there. He graduated from Davidson College, where he became a member of Phi Beta Kappa, and later attended Harvard as a Woodrow Wilson scholar. Mr. Stuart has been awarded the Howard Willet Prize for a summer's work on poetry, the Dylan Thomas Award of the Poetry Society of America, and a grant from the National Foundation on the Arts and Humanities. From 1961 to 1965 he taught in the English Department at the College of William and Mary, then became an Assistant Professor at Washington and Lee University in Lexington, Virginia, where he and his wife and their young son make their home. However, the winter of 1968–69 was spent in Vermont at Middlebury College, where Mr. Stuart was a visiting lecturer.

A Note on the Type

The text of this book was set in Monotype Bulmer. This distinguished type face is a competent recutting of a type long famous in the history of English printing that was designed and cut by William Martin about 1790 for William Bulmer of the Shakespeare Press. In design, it is all but a modern face, with vertical stress, sharp differentiation between the thick and thin strokes, and nearly flat serifs. The decorative italic shows the influence of Baskerville, whose pupil Martin was.

The book was composed, printed, and bound by Kingsport Press, Inc., Kingsport, Tennessee. Design by Betty Anderson.